THE Group® PRAISE & Worship SONGBOOK

Accompaniment Book

Companion Products:
Lyrics Book
Lyrics Transparencies
Split-Channel Cassette, Volumes 1–4
Split-Channel Compact Disc, Volumes 1–4

Group®

Loveland, Colorado

The Group Praise & Worship Songbook—Accompaniment
Copyright © 1994 Group Publishing, Inc.

Credits
Compiled and edited by Jennifer Root Wilger and Pam Clifford
Engraved and arranged by Craig Alea and Eric Shanfelt
Interior designed by Lisa Smith
Cover designed by Liz Howe

Library of Congress Cataloging-in-Publication Data
The group praise and worship accompaniment book / [compiled and
 edited by Jennifer Wilger and Pam Clifford].
  p. of music.
  Includes indexes.
  ISBN 1-55945-268-4
  1. Hymns, English. I. Wilger, Jennifer Root. II. Clifford, Pam.
III. Title: Group praise and worship accompaniment book.
M2117.G84 1994   94-20673
                                                   CIP
                                                    M

11 10 9 8 7 6 5 4   04 03 02 01 00 99 98 97 96
Printed in the United States of America.

More Precious Than Silver

Words and Music by Lynn DeShazo/Arranged by Eric Shanfelt

Lord, you are more pre - cious than sil - ver.

Lord, you are more cost - ly than gold.

Lord, you are more beau - ti - ful than dia - monds, and

noth- ing I___ de - sire com- pares with you.___

The Group Praise & Worship Songbook

Let the People Praise

Words and Music by James Ward/Arranged by Craig Alea

he_ a-lone is reign-ing o - ver us;_____ let the peo- ple praise the Lord;_
praise the Son who died to save___ us;_____

sov - 'reign God and King vic- to - ri- ous!_____
praise_ him for the call he gave__ us!_____ Let them praise, let them praise!

TRY THIS ▶ ▶ ▶   Each time you sing the chorus, clap on the off-beat (beats 2 and 4 of each measure).

Seek Ye First

Words and Music by Karen Lafferty/Arranged by Eric Shanfelt

TRY THIS ▶ ▶ ▶   Have the women sing the "Hallelujah" descant printed above each line while the men sing the verses.

I Will Call Upon the Lord

Words and Music by Michael O'Shields/Arranged by Eric Shanfelt

The Group Praise & Worship Songbook

of my sal-va-tion be ex-alt-ed. The alt-ed.

TRY THIS ▶▶▶ Have the women echo on the chorus.

5 Emmanuel
Words and Music by Bob McGee/Arranged by Eric Shanfelt

Em-man-u-el,_____ Em-man-u-el,_____ his name is called_____

Em-man-u-el._____ God with us,_____ re-vealed in us,_____

his name is called_____ Em-man-u-el._____

The Group Praise & Worship Songbook

Psalm 100

Arranged by Craig Alea

Psalm 103

Words and Music by Bob Stromberg/Arranged by Craig Alea

The Group Praise & Worship Songbook

TRY THIS ▶ ▶ ▶ Sing through the song once, then play it through a second time as people pray silently. Sing it a third time to celebrate God's forgiveness!

Lord, I Lift Your Name on High

Music by Rick Founds/Arranged by Craig Alea

The Group Praise & Worship Songbook

Ah, Lord God

Words and Music by Kay Chance/Arranged by Craig Alea

great and might-y God, great in coun-sel and might-y in deed,

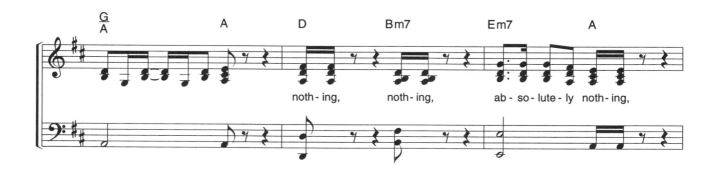

noth-ing, noth-ing, ab-so-lute-ly noth-ing,

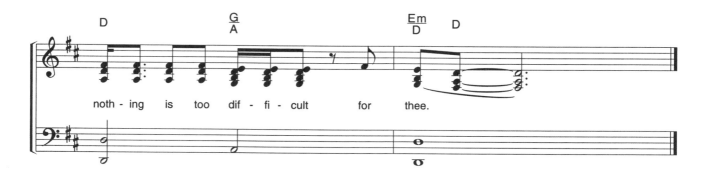

noth-ing is too dif-fi-cult for thee.

TRY THIS ▶ ▶ ▶   Sing this song at a moderate tempo. You'll have a "difficult" time singing if you go too fast!

From the Rising of the Sun

Author Unknown/Arranged by Craig Alea

Abba, Father

Words and Music by Carey Landry/Arranged by Eric Shanfelt

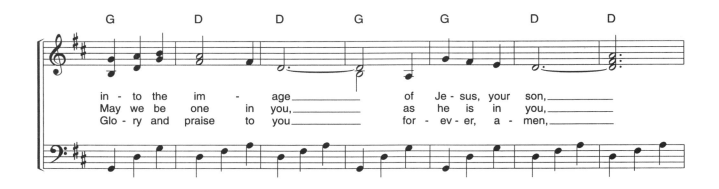

in - to the im - age _____ of Je - sus, your son, _____
May we be one in you, _____ as he is in you, _____
Glo - ry and praise to you _____ for - ev - er, a - men, _____

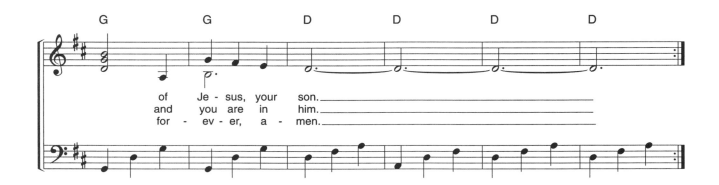

of Je - sus, your son. _____
and you are in him. _____
for - ev - er, a - men. _____

Move up a key each time through the song. Also, start out softly and build volume to the end. To move up a key, use the following chords: The second time through replace the chords D, G, and A with E flat, A flat, and B flat. The third time through use E, A, and B. The fourth time through use F, B flat, and C.

Lord of All

Words and Music by Steve Israel and Gerrit Gustafson/Arranged by Craig Alea

Je-sus Christ_ is the Lord of all, Lord of all_ the_ earth, Je-sus Christ_ is the Lord of all,

Lord of all_ the_ earth; Je-sus Christ_ is the Lord of all, Lord of all_ the_ earth,

Je-sus Christ_ is the Lord of all, Lord of all_ the_ earth._ On-ly one God_

o-ver the na-tions, on-ly one Lord_ of all; in

The Group Praise & Worship Songbook

All That I Need

Words and Music by John Paul/Arranged by Craig Alea

1. All that I need is you, all that I need is you;
2. My on-ly hope is you, my on-ly hope is you;
3. My on-ly peace is you, my on-ly peace is you;
4. My on-ly joy is you, my on-ly joy is you;

from ear-ly in the morn - ing till late at night
from ear-ly in the morn - ing till late at night
from ear-ly in the morn - ing till late at night
from ear-ly in the morn - ing till late at night

all that I need is you.
my on-ly hope is you.
my on-ly peace is you.
my on-ly joy is you.

5. All that I need is you, all that I need is you; from

The Group Praise & Worship Songbook

More Love, More Power

Words and Music by Jude Del Hierro/Arranged by Craig Alea

The Group Praise & Worship Songbook

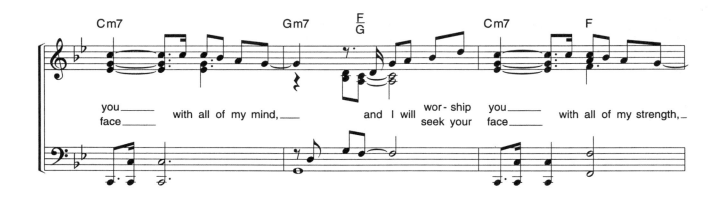

you_____ with all of my mind,____ and I will wor-ship you_____ with all of my strength,_
face_____ with all of my mind,____ seek your face_____

for you are my Lord._____ You are____ my

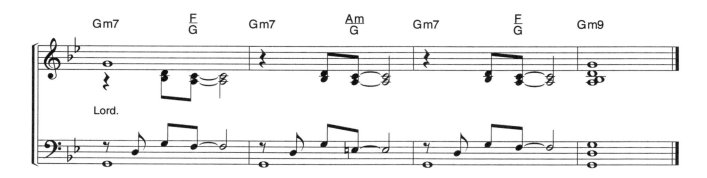

Lord.

TRY THIS ▶ ▶ ▶ Have the women echo on "more love" and "more power," then join the men on "more of you in my life."

Awesome God

Words and Music by Rich Mullins/Arranged by Eric Shanfelt

As the Deer

Words and Music by Martin Nystrom/Arranged by Eric Shanfelt

1. As the deer pant-eth for the wa-ter, so my soul long-eth af-ter thee.
2. You're my friend and you are my bro-ther, e-ven though you are a king.
3. I want you more than gold or sil-ver, on-ly you can sat-is-fy.

You a-lone are my heart's de-sire, __ and I long to wor - ship thee.
I love you more than an - y o-ther, so much more than an - y - thing.
You a-lone are the real joy gi-ver and the ap - ple of my eye.

You a-lone are my strength, my shield; to you a-lone may my spir-it yield.

You a-lone are my heart's de-sire, __ and I long to wor - ship thee.

The Group Praise & Worship Songbook

Soften My Heart

Words and Music by Graham Kendrick/Arranged by Craig Alea

Sof-ten my heart, Lord,_____ sof-ten my heart_____ from all in-dif-f'rence_____ set me a-part._____ To feel your com-pas-sion,_____ to weep with your tears;_____ come sof-ten my heart, O Lord, sof-ten my heart._____

The Group Praise & Worship Songbook

Beautiful

Words and Music by Dennis Cleveland/Arranged by Craig Alea

The Group Praise & Worship Songbook

A Shield About Me

Words by Donn Thomas/Music by Donn Thomas and Charles Williams/Arranged by Craig Alea

TRY THIS ▶ ▶ ▶ Have the women sing the "hallelujahs" in parentheses.

Soul's Celebration

Words and Music by Terry K. Dittmer/Arranged by Craig Alea

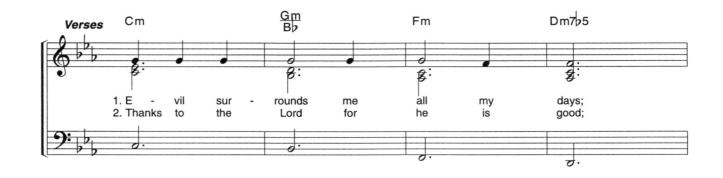

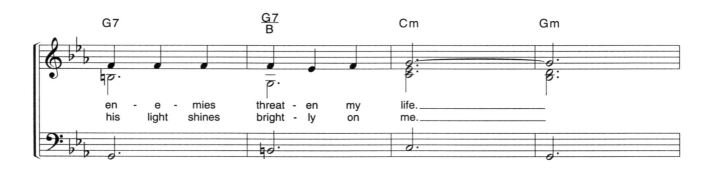

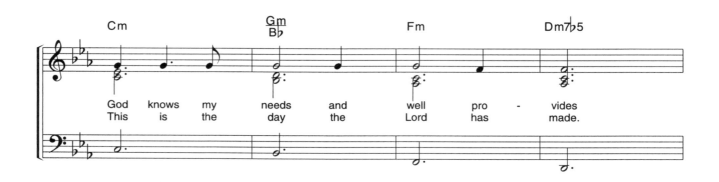

He Is Jehovah

Words and Music by Betty Jean Robinson/Arranged by Craig Alea

The Group Praise & Worship Songbook

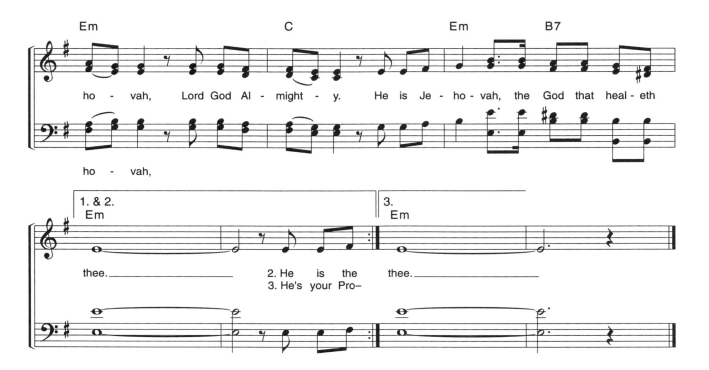

ho - vah, Lord God Al - might - y. He is Je - ho - vah, the God that heal - eth
ho - vah,

1. & 2. Em / **3.** Em

thee. _____
2. He is the thee. _____
3. He's your Pro—

Jehovah is an English translation for the Hebrew name of God, "Yahweh." You can read about the name "Jehovah-Shalom" (the Lord is peace) in Judges 6:24 and the name "Jehovah-Jireh" (the Lord provides) in Genesis 22:8, 14.

God Is So Good
Author Unknown/Arranged by Eric Shanfelt

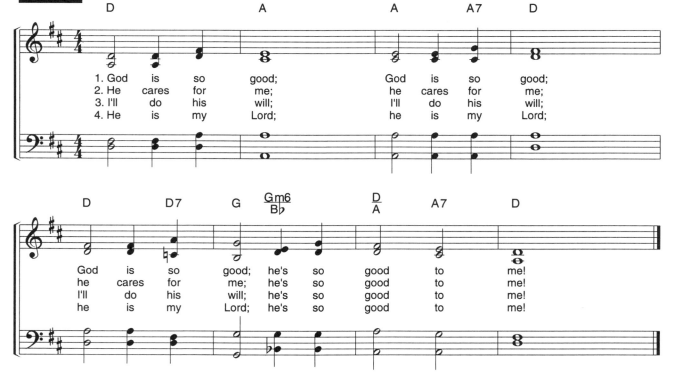

1. God is so good; God is so good;
2. He cares for me; he cares for me;
3. I'll do his will; I'll do his will;
4. He is my Lord; he is my Lord;

God is so good; he's so good to me!
he cares for me; he's so good to me!
I'll do his will; he's so good to me!
he is my Lord; he's so good to me!

Spirit Song

Words and Music by John Wimber/Arranged by Craig Alea

The Group Praise & Worship Songbook

Give Thanks

Words and Music by Henry Smith/Arranged by Eric Shanfelt

The Group Praise & Worship Songbook

TRY THIS ▶ ▶ ▶   Sing the song through once. Then play it through as people stand and spontaneously share things they're thankful for. Sing the song again, then pray and thank God together for all his blessings.

On Eagles' Wings

Words based on Psalm 91/Music by Michael Joncas/Arranged by Eric Shanfelt

Verse 1

1. You who dwell in the shel- ter of the Lord, who a - bide in his sha- dow for life, say to the Lord, "My re - fuge, my rock in whom I trust!" And he will

Chorus raise you up on ea - gles' wings, bear you on the breath of dawn, make you to shine_ like the sun, and hold you in_ the_ palm of his hand. 2. The

always cont. to next vs

The Group Praise & Worship Songbook

Jesus, Name Above All Names

Words and Music by Naida Hearn/Arranged by Craig Alea

The Group Praise & Worship Songbook

Brothers and Sisters in Christ

Words and Music by Terry Dittmer/Arranged by Craig Alea

1. Sing Al-le-lu-ia! A-men!_____ Let your prayers and your prais-es as-
2. Man walked a-lone and in need,_____ with-out faith, hope or prom-ise or
3. Lord, teach us how to pro-claim_____ all your good-ness, your love and your

cend._____ Lift up your voic-es and sing_____ to our
creed;_____ wan-der-ing aim-less-ly lost_____ un-a-
name!_____ Lord, teach us how to for-give,_____ and in

Lord God, our Sav-ior and King!_____ Here brought to-geth-er by
ware of the stag-ger-ing cost;_____ that God in his mer-cy would
love, teach us Lord, how to live._____ Rais-ing our voic-es in

grace,_____ we are gath-ered as friends in this place._____
save_____ all his peo-ple from death and the grave._____ And as-
song,_____ help us tell all the world we be-long._____

The Group Praise & Worship Songbook

Brand New Song

Words from Psalm 98/Music by Paula J. Meyer/Arranged by Craig Alea

1. Sing to the Lord_____ a brand new song; he has done won - der - ful things._____ He is a God____ of sal - va - - - tion; he is a right - eous King!

2. Sing to the Lord_____ a brand new song; he has the vic - to - ry._____ He has de - clared____ his faith - ful - ness; he is a lov - ing King.

Oh, break forth in praise___ and sing joy - ful - ly!____ Play with the trum - pet and horn.

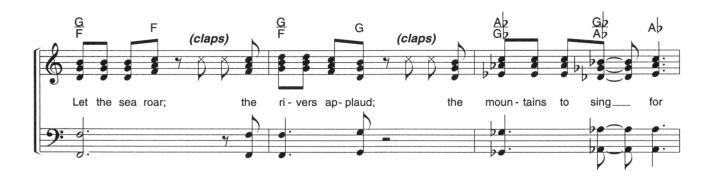

Let the sea roar; the ri- vers ap- plaud; the moun- tains to sing____ for

joy! Let the sea roar; the ri- vers ap- plaud; the

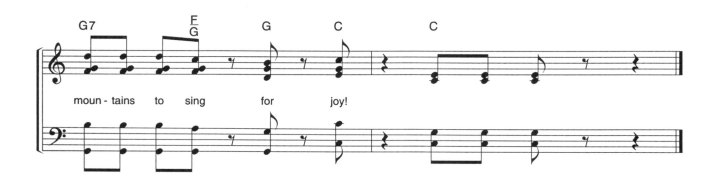

moun- tains to sing for joy!

TRY THIS ▶ ▶ ▶ The words to this song are based on Psalm 98. Read the psalm, then sing it!

Great Is the Lord

Words and Music by Michael W. Smith and Deborah D. Smith/Arranged by Eric Shanfelt

The Group Praise & Worship Songbook

Hear, Oh Israel

Words from Deuteronomy 6:4-5/Author Unknown/Arranged by Eric Shanfelt

Hear, oh Is - ra - el, the Lord our God is one Lord.

1. You shall love the Lord your God with all your heart.
2. You shall love the Lord your God with all your soul.
3. You shall love the Lord your God with all your mind.

(Echo)

4. You shall love the Lord your God with all your strength.

(Echo)

Our God Reigns

Words and Music by Leonard E. Smith Jr./Arranged by Craig Alea

The Group Praise & Worship Songbook

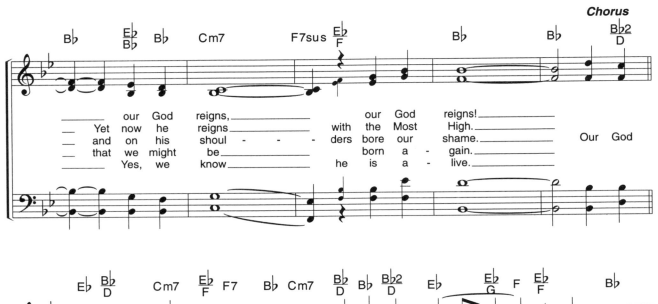

TRY THIS ▶ ▶ ▶ Build volume on each verse. When you reach the last chorus, sing "He's alive," instead of "Our God reigns."

The Group Praise & Worship Songbook

Lord, Be Glorified

Words and Music by Bob Kilpatrick/Arranged by Eric Shanfelt

The Group Praise & Worship Songbook

Here I Am, Lord

Words from Isaiah 6/Music by Dan Schutte/Arranged by Eric Shanfelt

Verses

1. I, the Lord of sea and sky, I have heard my people cry. All who dwell in dark and sin my hand will save. I who made the stars of night, I will make their darkness bright. Who will bear my light to them? Whom shall I send?

2. I, the Lord of snow and rain, I have borne my people's pain. I have wept for love of them. They turn away. I will break their hearts of stone, give them hearts for love alone. I will speak my word to them. Whom shall I send?

3. I, the Lord of wind and flame, I will tend the poor and lame. I will set a feast for them. My hand will save. Finest bread I will provide till their hearts be satisfied. I will give my life to them. Whom shall I send?

The Group Praise & Worship Songbook

Step by Step

Music by Beaker/Arranged by Craig Alea

O God, you are my God, and I will ev-er praise you. O God, you are my God, and I will ev-er praise you. I will seek you in the morn-ing, and I will learn to walk in your ways, and step by step you'll lead me, and I will fol-low you all of my days. O days.

The Group Praise & Worship Songbook

The Greatest Thing

Words and Music by Mark Pendergrass/Arranged by Craig Alea

The Group Praise & Worship Songbook

Canticle of the Sun

Words based on "Song of Brother Sun" by St. Francis of Assisi/Music by Marty Haugen/Arranged by Craig Alea

The heav- ens are tell- ing the glo- ry of God, ____ and all cre- a- tion is shout- ing for joy; ____ come, dance in the for- est, come, play in the field, ____ and sing, sing to the glo- ry of the Lord! ____

1. Sing to the
2. Praise to the
3. Praise to the
4. Praise to the
5. Sing to the
6. Praise to our

sun, the bring- er of day, he car- ries the light of the Lord in his
wind, that blows through the trees, the seas might- y storms, the gen- tl- est
rain, that wa- ters our fields, and bless- es our crops so all the earth
fire, who gives us his light, the warmth of the sun to bright- en our
earth, who makes life to grow, the crea- tures you made to let your life
death, that makes our life real, the know- ledge of loss that helps us to

The Group Praise & Worship Songbook

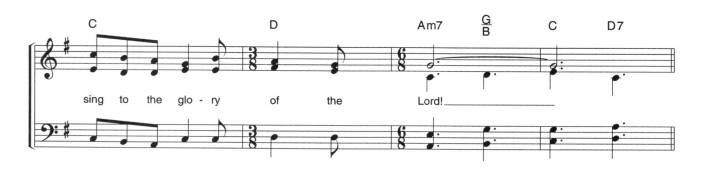

sing to the glo - ry of the Lord!

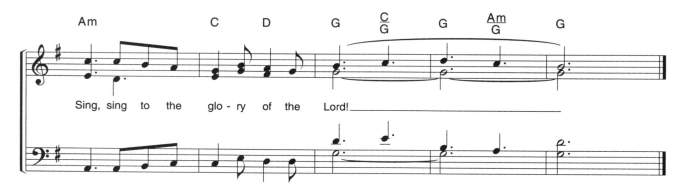

Sing, sing to the glo - ry of the Lord!

 ▶ ▶ ▶

This song lends itself well to creative movement. Before your worship time, assign two or three people to each verse. Have each pair or trio come up with movements to go with the words. Your movements can be as simple or elaborate as you want. Review each group's movements and practice them before your worship time.

Change My Heart, Oh God

Words and Music by Eddie Espinosa/Arranged by Eric Shanfelt

The Group Praise & Worship Songbook

Christ in Me

Words based on Philippians 1:21/Music by Gary Garcia/Arranged by Craig Alea

The Group Praise & Worship Songbook

Holy Ground

Words and Music by Geron Davis/Arranged by Craig Alea

The Group Praise & Worship Songbook

Father, I Adore You

Words and Music by Terrye Coelho/Arranged by Eric Shanfelt

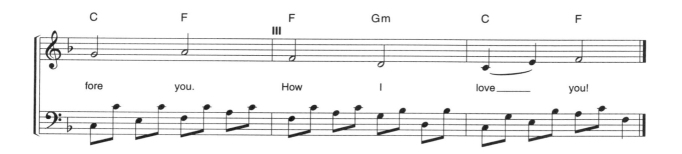

Lyrics:
1. Fa - ther,
2. Je - sus, I a - dore you, lay my life be -
3. Spir - it,

fore you. How I love ____ you!

TRY THIS ▶ ▶ ▶   Sing this song in a round. Have a group start at each Roman numeral.

The Group Praise & Worship Songbook

Holy, Holy

Words and Music by Jimmy Owens/Arranged by Eric Shanfelt

1. Ho - ly, ho - ly, ho - ly, ho - ly, ho - ly, ho - ly, _____ Lord God Al - might - y; and we
2. Gra - cious Fa - ther, gra - cious Fa - ther, we're so blest to be your child - ren, gra - cious Fa - ther; and we
3. Pre - cious Je - sus, pre - cious Je - sus, we're so glad that you've re - deemed us, pre - cious Je - sus; and we
4. Ho - ly Spir - it, Ho - ly Spir - it, come and fill our hearts a - new, Ho - ly Spir - it; and we
5. Ho - ly, ho - ly, ho - ly, ho - ly, ho - ly, ho - ly, _____ Lord God Al - might - y; and we
6. Hal - le - lu - jah, hal - le - lu - jah, hal - le - lu - jah, _____ hal - le - lu - jah, and we

lift our hearts be - fore_ you as a to - ken of our love, ho - ly, ho - ly, ho - ly, ho - ly.
lift our heads be - fore_ you as a to - ken of our love, gra - cious Fa - ther, gra - cious Fa - ther.
lift our hands be - fore_ you as a to - ken of our love, pre - cious Je - sus, pre - cious Je - sus.
lift our voice be - fore_ you as a to - ken of our love, Ho - ly Spir - it, Ho - ly Spir - it.
lift our hearts be - fore_ you as a to - ken of our love, ho - ly, ho - ly, ho - ly, ho - ly.
lift our hearts be - fore_ you as a to - ken of our love, hal - le - lu - jah, hal - le - lu - jah.

The Joy of the Lord

Words and Music by Alliene G. Vale/Arranged by Craig Alea

1. The joy___ of the Lord___ is my strength; the
2. He gives me liv-ing wa-ter and I thirst no more; he
3. He heals the bro-ken - heart-ed and they cry no more; he

joy___ of the Lord___ is my strength; the
gives me liv-ing wa-ter and I thirst no more; he
heals the bro-ken - heart-ed and they cry no more; he

joy___ of the Lord___ is my strength; the___
gives me liv-ing wa-ter and I thirst no more; the___
heals the bro-ken - heart-ed and they cry no more; the___

joy___ of the Lord___ is my strength._____
joy___ of the Lord___ is my strength._____
joy___ of the Lord___ is my strength._____

TRY THIS ▶ ▶ ▶   For an extra dose of joy, replace the words with "ha-ha's." You can also add your own verses, such as "If you want joy, you must *(name an action)* for it."

The Group Praise & Worship Songbook

There Is a Redeemer

Words and Music by Melody Green/Arranged by Craig Alea

1. There is a Re - deem - er, Je - sus, God's own son;___
2. Je - sus, my Re - deem - er, name a - bove all names;___
3. When I stand in Glo - ry, I will see his face;___

pre - cious Lamb of God, Mes - si - ah, Ho - - ly One.
pre - cious Lamb of God, Mes - si - ah, O___ for sin - ners slain.
there I'll serve my King for - ev - er in___ that ho - ly place.

Thank you, oh, my Fa - ther, for giv - ing us your son,___ and

leav - ing your spir - it 'til the work___ on___ earth is done.

The Group Praise & Worship Songbook

44 How Majestic Is Your Name

Words and Music by Michael W. Smith/Arranged by Eric Shanfelt

O Lord, our Lord, how ma-jes-tic is your name in all the earth! O Lord, our Lord, how ma-jes-tic is your name in all the earth! O Lord, we praise your name! O Lord, we mag-ni-fy your name. Prince of Peace, Might-y God, O Lord God Al-might-y!

TRY THIS ▶ ▶ ▶   Clap twice after you sing "all the earth."

The Group Praise & Worship Songbook

Create in Me

Words and Music by Mary Rice Hopkins/Arranged by Craig Alea

City of God

Music by Dan Schutte, S.J./Arranged by Craig Alea

Bless God

Words and Music by Carman and John Rosasco/Arranged by Craig Alea

Bless God for all he's done! Bless God for
voice in un-i-ty, one voice of

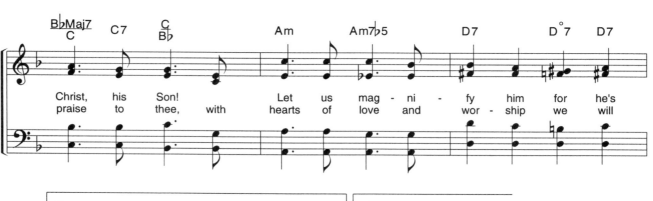

Christ, his Son! Let us mag-ni-fy him for he's
praise to thee, with hearts of love and wor-ship we will

1.
ho-ly, ho-ly! One

2.
sing, "Bless God!"

The Group Praise & Worship Songbook

As We Gather

Words and Music by Mike Fay and Tom Coomes/Arranged by Craig Alea

As we gath-er may___ your Spir-it work with-in us,

as we gath-er may___ we glo-ri-fy your name.___

Know-ing well that as___ our hearts be-gin to wor-ship,

we'll be blessed be-cause___ we came,___

we'll be blessed be-cause___ we came.

TRY THIS ▶▶▶ Sing this song as an opening for your meeting or worship service.

The Group Praise & Worship Songbook

Open Our Eyes

Words and Music by Bob Cull/Arranged by Eric Shanfelt

O-pen our eyes, Lord; we want to see Je - sus;
O-pen our ears, Lord; and help us to lis - ten.

to reach out and touch him and say that we love
O - pen our eyes,

him. Lord; we want to see Je - sus.

Our God Is Lifted Up

Words and Music by Tim Smith/Arranged by Craig Alea

The Group Praise & Worship Songbook

Humble Thyself in the Sight of the Lord

Words and Music by Bob Hudson/Arranged by Eric Shanfelt

The Group Praise & Worship Songbook

I Exalt Thee

Words and Music by Pete Sanchez Jr./Arranged by Eric Shanfelt

This Is the Day

Words and Music by Les Garrett/Arranged by Eric Shanfelt

The Group Praise & Worship Songbook

We Will Glorify

Words and Music by Twila Paris/Arranged by Eric Shanfelt

The Group Praise & Worship Songbook

Bless the Name of Jesus

Words and Music by Carman/Arranged by Craig Alea

Bless the name of Je-sus, praise the name of Je-sus,

sing un-to the King____ of Is-ra-el.____

Bless the name of Je-sus, praise the name of Je-sus,

sing un-to the King____ of Is-ra-el.____ And I sing

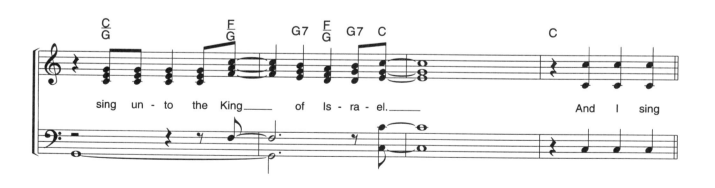

The Group Praise & Worship Songbook

TRY THIS ▶ ▶ ▶ Have participants raise and lower their arms each time you sing "glory."

56 Come and Sing Praises

Words and Music by Paul Neale Lessard/Arranged by Craig Alea

We Bow Down

Words and Music by Twila Paris/Arranged by Craig Alea

1. You are Lord of cre-a-tion and Lord of my life,
Lord of the land and the sea.
You were Lord of the heav-ens be-fore there was time,
and Lord of all lords you will be!
We bow

King of cre-a-tion and King of my life,
King of the land and the sea.
You were King of the heav-ens be-fore there was time,
and King of all kings you will be!

The Group Praise & Worship Songbook

Come to the Water

Words and Music by Paul Neale Lessard/Arranged by Craig Alea

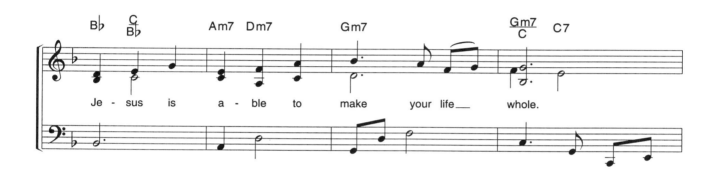

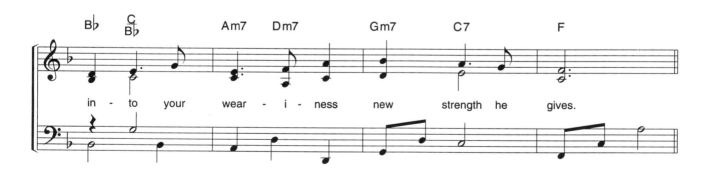

The Group Praise & Worship Songbook

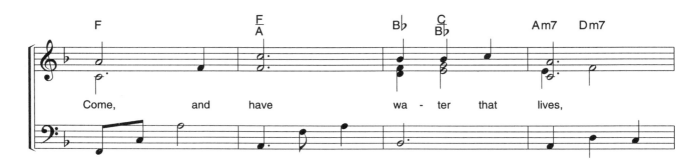

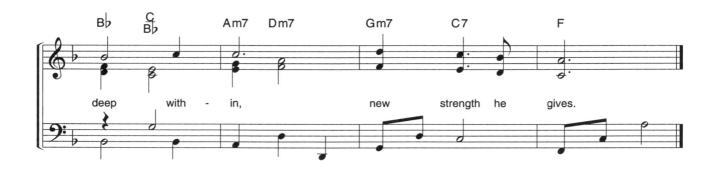

TRY THIS ▶ ▶ ▶   Sing through the melody, then the descant. Then form two groups and sing them both at the same time. You can use the accompaniment for either part.

I Sing Praises

Words and Music by Terry MacAlmon/Arranged by Craig Alea

The Group Praise & Worship Songbook

I Will Celebrate

Words and Music by Linda Duvall/Arranged by Eric Shanfelt

The Group Praise & Worship Songbook

61 What a Mighty God We Serve

Author Unknown/Arranged by Craig Alea

The Group Praise & Worship Songbook

You Are My Hiding Place

Words and Music by Michael Ledner/Arranged by Craig Alea

TRY THIS ▶▶▶ Sing through the song once. Then form two groups. Have the second group start singing, "You are my hiding place" after the first group sings, "Whenever I am afraid, I will trust in you."

In His Time

Words and Music by Diane Ball/Arranged by Craig Alea

1. In his time (in his time), in his time (in his time), he makes
2. In your time (in your time), in your time (in your time), you make

all things beau - ti - ful in his time (in his time). Lord, please
all things beau - ti - ful in your time (in your time). Lord, my

show me ev - 'ry day as you're teach - ing me your way, that you
life to you I bring; as may each song I have to sing be to

do just what you say in your time (in your time).
you a love - ly thing in your time (in your time).

The Group Praise & Worship Songbook

64 Isn't He?

Words and Music by John Wimber/Arranged by Craig Alea

The Group Praise & Worship Songbook

God Is Good

Words and Music by Morris Chapman/Arranged by Craig Alea

God is good (God is good) all the time!___
___ (all the time!) God is good (God is good)
all the time!___ (all the time!) Well, he's filled___

The Group Praise & Worship Songbook

TRY THIS ▶ ▶ ▶   Have your worship leader sing, "God is good all the time" and have the congregation echo. Then sing together on "Well, he's filled with compassion, and his mercies are everlasting!"

Jehovah-Jireh

Words and Music by Merla Watson/Arranged by Craig Alea

66

Je - ho - vah Ji - reh, my Pro - vid - er, his grace is suf - fi - cient for __ me, for me, __ for me;

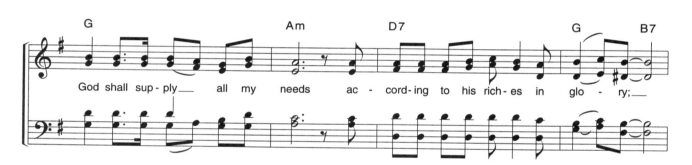

Je - ho - vah Ji - reh, my Pro - vid - er, his grace is suf - fi - cient for __ me. My

God shall sup - ply __ all my needs ac - cord - ing to his rich - es in glo - ry; __

he gives his an - gels __ charge o - ver me, Je - ho - vah Ji - reh cares __ for __

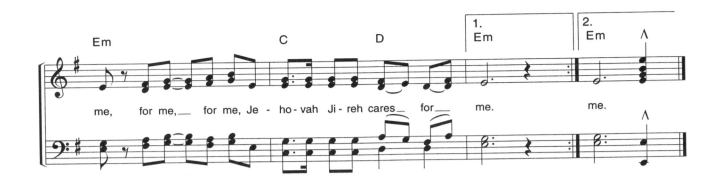

me, for me,___ for me, Je - ho-vah Ji - reh cares___ for___ me.   me.

Explain that Jehovah-Jireh means "the Lord provides." When God provided a ram for Abraham to sacrifice in place of his son, Isaac, Abraham named the place "Jehovah-Jireh." See Genesis 22 for more details.

I Love You, Lord

Words and Music by Laurie Klein/Arranged by Eric Shanfelt

I love you, Lord,___ and I lift my voice___ to wor-ship

you; O my soul, re-joice! Take joy, my King,___ in___

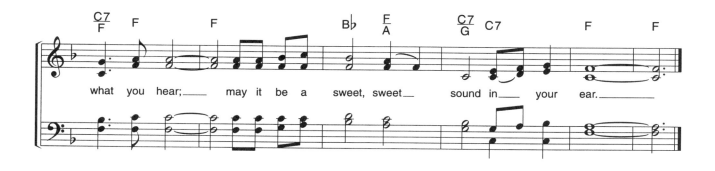

what you hear;___ may it be a sweet, sweet___ sound in___ your ear.___

The Group Praise & Worship Songbook

The Battle Belongs to the Lord

Words and Music by Jamie Owens-Collins/Arranged by Craig Alea

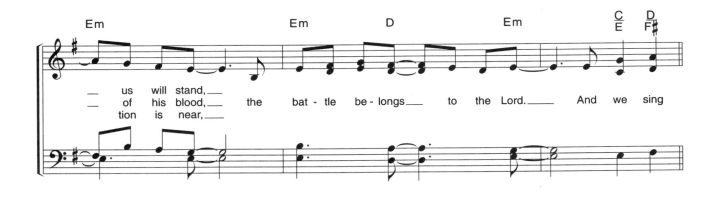

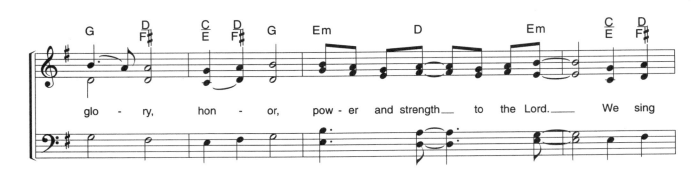

The Group Praise & Worship Songbook

glo - ry,   hon - or,   pow - er and strength__ to the Lord.___

2. When the
3. When your

pow - er   and strength_____ to   the   Lord._____

Shine, Jesus, Shine

Words and Music by Graham Kendrick/Arranged by Craig Alea

1. Lord, the light of your love is shin-ing, in the midst of the dark-ness, shin-ing: Je-sus, Light of the world, shine up-on us; set us free by the truth you now bring us— shine on___ me, shine on___ me.
2. Lord, I come to your awe-some pres-ence, from the sha-dows in-to your ra-di-ance; by your blood I may en-ter your bright-ness: search me, try me, con-sume all my dark-ness— shine on___ me, shine on___ me.
3. As we gaze on your king-ly bright-ness so our fa-ces dis-play your like-ness, ev-er chang-ing from glo-ry to glo-ry: mir-rored here, may our lives tell your sto-ry— shine on___ me, shine on___ me.

Create in Me a Clean Heart

Words from Psalm 51/Arranged by Eric Shanfelt

Create in me a clean heart, O God, and renew a right spirit within me. Cre–

Cast me not away from thy presence, O Lord, and take not thy Holy Spirit from me. Restore unto

me the joy of thy salvation, and renew a right spirit within me.

The Group Praise & Worship Songbook

CHURCH

ENCOURAGEMENT

GOD

The Group Praise & Worship Songbook